MY MAGNUM OPUS

My Magnum Opus

~

YUSUF MIFSUD

RESOURCE *Publications* · Eugene, Oregon

MY MAGNUM OPUS

Resource Publications
An Imprint of Wipf and Stock Publishers
199 W. 8th Ave., Suite 3
Eugene, OR 97401

www.wipfandstock.com

PAPERBACK ISBN: 978-1-6667-8943-0
HARDCOVER ISBN: 978-1-6667-8944-7
EBOOK ISBN: 978-1-6667-8945-4

VERSION NUMBER 09/25/23

Contents

I Built a City Last Week

Cars like collectible rings, twenty on each hand.
Little people staring up in confusion, little conversations too.
My apartment sunk into the seaside.

I watched it erode into the face of a smile in the sand.
Children raced, sweat and all, pointing at the sight.

All the lights snuck behind the electrical wiring.
A tsunami visited the shore, roughly shaking its hand.

Children slew, sweat and all, like a basket of beads drops to the
    ground.

—it was almost in slow motion.

One light persisted, its flicker of light fighting for air.
A coastal home with my name glazed on the windows.

Peering inside, my mother was cooking like a famous chef.
She was laughing at the chaos of it all, it did not shake her.

So, I sat with a book and a pen, covering the entire beach.
We lit up the entire city.

Just a mother, her son and a tsunami.

Apple Pie

Doughy exterior, slightly undercooked.
Knives as insults through the center, check for blemishes.
Has the apple ripened in the heat of it all?

Calloused with crust like snowflakes and frostbite.
Each puncture hardened the dough yet softened the apple sludge.
Pudge became rock, and rock birthed shells.

I keep coming back to the beachside,
It has a lyrical way of pulling me back toward buoys.

Apple met sand, encrusting it like a big fat ring,
but the contents were stubborn, for it remained all gooey.

—So many centuries.

Archaeologists discovered what they thought was the fossil of a
    boy.
Each sand particle flicking away with articulate tools and eyes.
The shore was very displeased, resentment through growling
    splashes,

But all they found was apple pie.

The Unremembering

White picket fences like swords,
Trophies displayed from many duels.

They protected poppies that cried cherry syrup,
Jiving to the peculiarities the garden presented.

But he looked on from the other side of the road,
Separated by a concoction of bitumen and loath.

—What was it?

The poppies squinted at him from a distance.

—What do you want?

He slowly slithered into the road's scars,
Melting into concrete.

With their leafy arms, the poppies pulled the grass like
     puppeteers.
Earth's axis pivoted, tilting the concrete toward the garden.

In each movement, the picket fence cheered as the poppies fought
     gravity.
By the time he reached the garden, he was not the same.

He was a poppy.

Wake Up

White beds, cousins of disfigured clouds.
Windows barred up by misadventure and years, and years.

"Silly child, you belong here, on these very tiles".

He contemplated with his bookshelf and couch, it stretched into
    a decade.
Reading old poetry and strange stories from a while ago.

—years and years.

Ears and ears, so many voices sinking into his scalp, drowning his
    cognitive functions.
Family functions like sipping poison at a morbidly slow rate.

Hair designs and clothes of shame, bleach that felt more appro-
    priate for a stomach.

You remind me of that white bed,
Sheets like chains stuck in clockwork encrusted in red,
Rust in my head balancing six legged men.

White bed.

I Wrote a Song to The Mountains

Gripping cliff faces with tar and compassion.
Just one more reason, I say.

The eucalyptus listened, reluctantly.
I used stones that lost their mothers to carve initials,
Into the eyes of the mountains.

Pain has a curious way of existing,
It lasts as long as you allow it.

So, I drenched leaves in anesthetics and lyrics,
Covering the two windows of the mountain.

I slowly put it to rest with a lullaby about two friends.
Stoic regret and glorious debt overtook in fret.

The mountain lay rest.

Apartments Sat Empty with the Sidewalk

I feel the uneven paint job, too many coats,
The one I wore with no pockets and a peaking hood.

—What was I doing at eighteen?

Theaters with perspective of a bat.
Why can't I keep it all out?

Sidewalks like hikes on a Saturday off,
I was dreading that one steep step on the pavement.

At one point I did not sweat as I do now,
Jackets read comfort, and eyes of prowl.

—A time of creation.

My life has become a strange story of an artist.
I never wanted a hollow apartment,

Or a vacant table with three fake plants,
Or an orange bulb coupled with some lamp.

I sat empty, on the sidewalk.

Sushi Store

Little stools and round tables.
A sharp gust, skies shyly blue.

The patrons filled with concern, even the bushes were
    questioning.

I could smell a brewery of six different cuisines, they were
    confused.

—What was I doing all the way in Sydney?

All the way, all the way.
All the while, something else was calling.
All the while, someone else is searching.
All the while, The Pacific is melting.

Feet only took me so far.
Shoes only served me so much.
Shirts only cooled me in March.

What skies can I have if I am in the gravel?
What stores can gift me, if I'll just unravel?

Not here.

Silhouette

Dear, dear, dear.
Johannes Vermeer.

Riled paint brush, haughty hands,
Blonde tail, and blue bands.

Eyes just marbles, and peril.
Het meisje met de parel.

Despair, Mechelen Inn.

Cracks cast at stone,
Dawn past the lower robe.

Strokes like cascading graves,
Auctions of passing stains,

—on canvas.

Silhouette.

I Give Me

Like cookie shards and lost remnants of fossilized dinosaurs.

Give, and give, and give.

The jar is empty, just glass.

So, I used my teeth to cut brand-new shards.
I cut my gums while I'm at it—after all,
It's glass.

When will I have a choc chip,
Melt in my teeth with grace and sweetness?

Will I give me a lid?
Like ones on jars as circles and rims?

Take, and take, and take.

Your stomach is all used up,
Your digestive system is tired, that's enough.

Take just one, not five, or nine.

Just one.

Hollywood Hell

Melrose, your bells chime like the church next to my last
    apartment.
I burnt my toast last week, it fumed back at me, barking for
    better.

I see my toaster in Hollywood.
Some unfitting apartment with a balcony not the same,
People with stitched up faces and wonky smiles on Sunset Blvd.

I see my family in Sydney.
Forgotten imagery in a mosaic, thousands and thousands of tiles.
Cousins who forgot my name, granted it back by Melrose.

—Melrose, Santa Monica, La Brea.

What will such luxuries grant the poorest hands?
What will such sanctuaries provide in convoluted paths?

So, we're back to Melrose.

I see an extinct species, just one left.
I'm wrapped in three blankets—toiled with tears.
Ink on paper as medicine in throats.

Hollywood.

I Never Existed

i.

A fake mirage, on a pop-up set, for an also fake film.
I saw it, I swear!

I watched myself from the lens of an abandoned camera.
Each frame blending to the next.
I disappeared ever so slowly.

The sand calmly eating the tripod for lunch.

—I was next.

So, I ran, feet competing with the mirage,
The mirage competing with homage.

But my face dissolved with the wind,
My hair gripping tightly to all my things.

—Tighter, and tighter, and tighter.

ii.

Well, I just grew thin,
Bones broke—needles and pins.
Memories churned in slots, casino machines.

Will I luck out this time?

'Take one more spin', I crave.

So, I move in frame, the ten second counter begins.

Green screens wipe ashes, from opaque to grim.

I was dragged to the sea, foamed mouths of shores.
Just cameras, galore.

iii.

The tide took me, once more.

—More, and more, and more.

Fish and chips for dinner at four,
Props and robes, we're candid as sores.

But running just took me back, at best.
I stood in frame,

That's where I lay rest.

You'll Probably Find Me Somewhere
in the Soil, After It Was All Written

I never considered being thirty.
Just one more decade.

I don't think I'll make it that far.
Each particle of my existence was channeled,
Spun like gold in a wheel for twenty.

—And yet, I'm not pliable.

My lids rest and throw me back to the beach.
I had a dream, I lived underwater with small whales and koi.

I did not drown, I spoke.
I did not frown, I wrote.

Can I go back?

—Just one last time, before I go.

Will they read along,
Or wait 'till I'm six feet below.

You'll probably find me somewhere in the soil, after it was all
    written.

Salted Rocks in The Maldives

I wanted to lay down, cut my scalp on the rocks,
Sink into the residue of my fluids.
Drink the gifts of the ocean, finish with a spoon of salt.

—Apply a medical concoction of salt and fish bones.

Stitches of nature, guppies admiring with wide eyes.
San Francisco is watching me from the shirt of a boy.
The Maldives, peering past the rocks with envy.

—Envy, envy, envy.

Bandaged head, guppies for pets and my companion a big red
     bridge.

"But I miss The Maldives", I yearned.

Waves with five fingers, each felt absent.
Waves with five fishes, each felt arrogant.

We bargained for hours over rocks and cuts,
A steep price past the anchoring metal of that bridge.
I dragged myself like luggage for hours,
Vehicles blaring at me.

—This was San Francisco.

I missed every cut, every burn, every touch
The white granulite gave me.

Swims with the guppies sometime later,
Touching cuts like sustenance, savor.

I can still hear the rocks and spoons waver.

Architecture

I am not a brand.
I am not transient.
I am an Empire.

I rebuild.

On the Cusp of Summer

Paddling toward the end of November.
Take me to December, I was almost a Scorpio.

Seventeen degrees in Leo, they say it brings inevitable fortune.

Fortune for what?

This whole time I just wanted a little house.
Timber serenading the rooftop's creatures,
Somber silencing the sounds of LA.

This whole time I just wanted a confidant.
Turning pages in anticipation, fingers faster than flight.
Twisting age in infatuation, years hastier than nights.

I waited on Dolby Theatre's stage, with the curtains and audio
    equipment.

They counseled me for some time, I fled with the stage lights.

There was something pulling me below the seating—and under.

—Just on the cusp of summer.

They're Starting to Notice Me

The Universe's long nails, fingers like towers.
Pointing at me through the stratosphere,
Shining a spotlight down, even the sun ran away.

So many eyes.

—Eyes, and eyes, and eyes.

I opened my books, and became a beacon,
Each letter called a new look.

Hooks as anchors at sea, pioneering my spirit,
My spirit aching for something else.

I rose through my beacon, I had so many questions.
The asteroids looked me right in the face,
Inspecting every lash and its taste.

But I had already been elected at fourteen, so they said.
Will it become too much for my head?

I already renovated my frontal lobe,
Will there be enough space for thrones?

—Frontal lobe, frontal lobe.

News articles and chatter, gossip and distasteful clatter.

"Will the boy from LA rise, or shatter?"

But the Universe never stopped pointing,

It did not matter.

Paint Me a Picture of a Small Townhouse with
a Bad Drainage System and Withered Grass

i.

I asked so many times, I was a beggar downtown.
Just fifty dollars to my name, and a spirit with crowns.

So, I rode a bus on the night before my birthday to an apartment.
Three hundred dollars to pocket.

No clue of my stay.
Double my age, kitchen counters like clay.

We moved from tiles, to carpet, then beds.
I was held up at my chest, no clothes, nor rest.
Sinking in brushes that frayed at their heads.

But the rest…

ii.

—The rest, the rest, all the rest.

The rest was seen in a studio apartment—at best.
No windows, just doors and strange ornaments.
Nitrite lungs and three hours of sleep, say less.

I suppose I died that night; my corpse is still there.
A drink in its hand and ten fingers on stairs,
Winding like willows at a townhouse with crests.

"Just paint me a picture atop my bedhead"

, I said.

iii.

But the drains showed no mercy, for they coughed out rain,
Granting a mosaic, missing tiles, missing land.
Stains on the grass married withering plants.

Three hundred dollars to pocket,
Sunbathe in lust, and towns and all of it.
Paintings in plight, we see none of it.

And just one broken vase.

—One broken vase.

Maybe If I Liked Beer

I should have just said yes when you asked,
I should have just kept on opaque masks.

I should have been less exuberant,
I should have been more subdued, and

Maybe you'd like the way I look more,
Maybe you like when I hide my core.

Maybe you'd run after me through woven crowds,
Maybe I'd have ran further in the sound.

Will I be more desirable if I just drink beer?
Will I be more tangible if I just sit here?

Could a lobotomy help sink my intellect?
Could stitches close my mouth—dissect?

What if I cooked to the center, filleted raw?
What if I peeled away each element with claws?

So, I see, I should just remain an autopsy.
So, see me away at sea after my biopsy.

Fish me with bait, beer at the end of the hook.
Fish me with a chorus, watch me look.

I should have, but I won't.

I won't.

I Was Destined

The stars keep telling me I am destined for more.
Twenty-third of November, two thousand and two, is when I was
    born,

Eleven fifty-nine at night.

I don't really know where I stand anymore.
I feel misplaced in Sydney, she wants me out.
I feel LA, who forbid me speaking aloud.

What about LA draws me close,
Maybe her pearls that quietly make one choke?

I don't really know what day I was born.
I feel deceptive numbers and shores.
I feel reflective waves abroad.

—Abroad, abroad, abroad.

My angel numbers pressured me further,
They say there is no way I can escape success,
They say I grow each time I digress.

—Eleven.

My Mother only believes in God,
But she said I was destined for more.

My Father doesn't believe in himself,
But even he said I was destined for wealth.

Everyone is in my ears at once,
Megaphone to my drums,
Numbing feelings on my thumbs.

The constellations cried to me one time,
I didn't quite match their stars and lines.
My soul was misplaced in a strange little rhyme.

So, I wrote on pages, sometimes two at night,
I collected letters, ink and long breathed sighs.
I collected retrospect, locked her away with goodbyes.

—Writing, and writing, and writing.

In a frenzy.

Why Did You Take All of Those Things?

Why did you take me on dates?
Why did you sleep with me—twice?
Why did you make me feel special?
Why did you make me feel heard for the first time?
Why did you swim with me at the beach?
Why did you take me for walks?
Why did you show me gardens, plants, and knowledge?
Why did you tell me I was cute?
Why did you tell me I was beautiful?
Why did you tell me goodnight each day?
Why did you talk with me for 30 days straight?
Why did you pursue me with no real end goal?
Was this all entirely premeditated?
Was this a means of using me for pleasure?
Was this experience all for you?
Was any of this ever for me?
Was I doomed from the very first message?
Was my fate laid bare before me?
Was I blinded by my own genuineness?
Am I too easy?
Am I too kind to the people I meet?
Am I too forgiving to the worst I see?
Am I too hopeful in humanity?
Will I ever reap what I sew?
Will you ever check up on me?
Will you remember my name?
Will you remember what you did to me?
Are you happy now?
Are you pleased with the outcome?
Are your urges satisfied?
But did you consider my intelligence?

But did you think I'll go away yet?
My presence is immortal.
My haunting lasts forever.

Chasing

I was far more pronounced, a vocalist.
I locked my balcony with such ease and confidence.

—Confidence, and confidence, and confidence.

What about ten years ago?
What about when I created a show?
What about how I encapsulated ten rows?

The sun quickly became medicinal.
Sitting became poisonous,
And blinds became blindfolds on my chest.

Dependent on the elements encasing my body,
My bedroom turned into a dictatorship.
The sheets commanding, I lay bare beneath them.
My mirrors casting spells that bound me to my own reflection.

I was moving too fast,
Stays in the bathroom left remnants of left on light bulbs,
Lays on the couch turned reverence into regret.

—Regret, and regret, and regret.

I was stagnant, yet in five places at once.
They watched on, as if at a football game
awaiting a penalty.

A penalty for my envious ambition.
A penalty for my loud disposition.
A penalty for my unsure fruition.

I showered my balcony with contemplation,
It shivered in the unforgiving cold.

But I cannot pay the price for insecurity.

I Cannot Seem to Grapple the Concept of a Life That Was Not Designed for Me

i.

I have a small sailboat resting in Peck Park.
A swing set with the quiet companionship of thrusting chains.
I watched each chain move—harshly jolting against one another.
I watched another boy take the life designed for me.

—All the way in Sydney.

So, I sang to my sailboat at two in the morning.
Not even the dew had opened its eyes,
Not even the stores unlocked their arms at this time.

But Peck Park was adamant on its stay.

"Change your concept, swallow your contempt."

He said, as his trees were gatekeeping the chain's safe haven.

My impurity oozed into the Indian Ocean, who carried my de-
    plorable soul,
Its head down and shameful eyes.

—All the way in Peck Park.

It was all meaningless semantics, for nothing would shift my
    timeline.

ii.

So, I went to the backyard—gloves and all.
I committed murder.
—Dismantled, disfigured.

The swing set pleaded with me for hours, presenting its case,
Chains for lawyers.

But I was persistent.

A designer, an architect, a marvel of creation.
Piece by piece, a swing set took flight to sea,
It was now a vessel.

The Indian Ocean was a non-traditionalist,
Each wave was a dice rolling with no finality,
And each cave provided a debate.

"Sydney is just a few kilometers away", so they'd say.

But the very same caves jeweled rocks and remains with
Rot that stared at me with faces carved with neglect.
The riptide curled its tibia into the algae,
Carefully spitting water from its mouth at me.

iii.

I grew a beard, and three holes in my shirt.

 Shark teeth swam to the surface, I used them for razors,
Algae for dinner.
—Peck Park, Peck Park.

Oh, what a sailboat she was.
I neared the harbor, defiant of suggestion.

Green and blue stripes, my initials carved into
The heart of the boat— she was mine.
But when she saw me, the sailboat ran behind shipment
   containers.

All I was left with was Peck Park.

—And my swing set.

I Remember Everything

But I wish I didn't.
I'm obsessed with retrospect,
I'm obsessed with lost respect.

But I wish I wasn't.
I miss the sand—oh the way it whipped my back,
Left me with a proceeding splash.

—Splash, splash, splash.

Take me to Santa Monica Beach,
She can clean me up.

Take me to the ER,
He can stitch me up.

Just don't leave me here, please.
Let me down, and do it slowly.
Write me a speech for my funeral,
Because I still remember everything.

—Can you?

I Spoke to a Coworker Today for Thirty Minutes, and It Was Enlightening

Is it better to have a conscience and no wheel, or a wheel and no
    conscience?
Either is misdirected, and yet we all mesh into either category.

He asked:

"On a scale from zero to one hundred, how confused are you?"

I was fast to say one hundred, my tongue directed me,
My mind moved at the same pace.

Complete confidence in my stance.

We all live in intrinsic levels of confusion, in every facet of our
    being.
There is no singular truth to the purpose of our meaning,
For such a thing is an unattainable concept.

I question how I look, chew, smile, move, talk and breathe.
I question these things from a personal, and third person
    standpoint.

I have ulterior motives,
I know you do too.

We are investigators by nature,
We are interrogators in flavor.

Then there's those who will answer:

"I am zero percent confused".

I detect insecurity, I used a magnifying glass and two eyes.
I detect submission to auto-pilot, roaming in meaningless daze.
I detect misery on a multitude of levels, masked by 'friends' and
    'fun'.

I can see you, right before me.
You cannot hide.

You would cease to exist with full clarity,
For your purpose of endeavor is dead.

Accept confusion,
Accept consciousness.

Marveled by All the Places

What could I do to get there?
Hair holding the sides of my face for dear life,
Tongues rolling smoke like hard candy at a candy store I saw in
    twenty thirteen.

I've never been so multifaceted in my sense of existing,
I am not in Sydney, but I am always here.

—Always, always, all ways.

Another poem about escapism, ink is controlling my fate.

I am a wand.
I am a spell.

I Live as a Nightmare and a Dream

My life is a juxtaposition in itself.
I swim in contemplation like a stingray,
I huddle beneath the sand and prey upon my thoughts.

I am a strong, ambitious adventurer,
Living in this rare opportunity of inquisition.
My art is my very own blessing,
My soul is the very fabric of its existence, for which I am grateful.

Everything I perceive is through a beautiful lens,
Everything I breathe, within trees and scents.

I am loving all of it,
Mesmerized by the horrors that only I can experience.
Everything is materialized into art, tangible appreciation.
I'm in love with the losses I take and the things I break,
I'm in touch with the wind, and clay, and the things I make.

Every second, I say, is my chance to create.
Living in LA and Sydney, all day.
Existing in awe of my apartment's gates.

I am a conscious creature of this place.
A mountain dweller, dreamer of cold winters,
Enveloped in numb hands and teeth that dance.

I'm digesting my minutes until I die,
Something that is real and inedible.

Something that is invaluable.

Taking Up

I'm a real person,
My portrayal is transparent, I show my guts.
They lay bare on the rocks, dinner for crabs.

Submission to standardized smiles,
Existing in the essence of another.
Solace in the exhilaration of a mile.

Something I cannot fathom.

Desensitized to providing and not receiving,
Realized by a gesture I give like no other.
I'm just like my mother.

I'm a beacon of misery,
Riddled in leaves that speak too much to their trees.
Cities who watch the suburbs, squinting with seethe.

—So, they say.

Misted oceans I appreciate,
My mother reminds me of kindness.
Her arms anchor silence.

She taught me so well,
For it is us who pay the price.

We are real people.

Purposeless Interactions

Stares, charades and no aim.
Eyes roll past the bayou like clay.

Clockwork,
No gears nor tame.

Relishing in Pain

Decayed like a candle,
Down to the wick in a few months.

Went from youthful to drunken so fast.
I miss those swims, goosebumps just thinking about them.

Glasses couldn't help my focus.
Thought I'd gain clarity—just soft bruising to my nose.

Thought more clocks could usher me to sleep,
They kept me up steep, 2am deep.

All of it under the shrug of 'whatever'.
What ever could I have done?

Late night shifts, I don't work for the dollar anymore.
Distracted by purposeless, inanimate materials.

I'm so much more than this awful fate,
My wax needs hardening in the day.

Don't want this struggle, I need it.

Pearl Farming

Dew fell from metal to concrete,
A son was chasing his mother's feet.
Riveted by words on talking streets,
The way they scream in pain to me.

Crocheted webs on my balcony,
Twisting a spindle of melancholy.
Shrewd in absence of symphonies,
I sang a song, I'm just off-key.

I forgot it all, left all behind,
Went to the shore, she took my mind.
In a clam it lay in silky peace,
I took the pearl, was just one piece.

So now we're back to my place,
I don't know how I keep my pace.
I'll probably fall soft, sleep it away,
Taking things slowly,

Just day by day.

In the Trenches

I sashay through crowds; I am a blanket.
My veil is weak, we're at a wedding,
And I am the bride.

My ignorance is havoc on a windy day,
Their eyes are watching from miles away,
And I am their pride.

I walk faster than sprinters, I am a marathon.
My stride is long, I'm in such a hurry.

—A hurry for what?

They told me I have so much time, time,
And time again.

Eyes are of essence, and time is repellent.
We're fighting for her, in a small-town play,
They want the part, but I want the day.

—All of it.

Second and Third

Always,
Just missing the mark.

A small tester of first, nothing more than that.
A small crest of yearn, I want more than that.

It's been years now.
I'm watching through a double mirror; she cackled back at me.
I'm watching past a puddled river; he sighed in agony.

They always say I'll get a break.

But when?
For what?

Once I've broken my hands and they've watched me rot?
Once I've woven my plans and they've famished my crops?

"Stop doing so much, stop eating this lunch." I tell myself.

But then what?

Become the monster under my bed who is complacency?
Become the man in my head that lacks any urgency?

I cannot stay still, I want to immerse myself in the experience,
The experience of being a human.

I cannot accept less, but less is looking right at me.

Hysteria

I broke into hysteria, 20 CDs worth of it.
Just a few months—minutes became topaz soaked in oil.
Sylvia Plath became my only confidant.

I used to only type my poetry, was on the go.
CDs included insight in the packaging.

Insight was kind some days.
On others, twirling my vision into inversion.

Kate Bush told me to do things for myself.
So, I used a pen instead to envision my threads.

Lana Del Rey told me to love the darkest moments, kiss them
    softly.
So, I capitalized on tragedy, instead of letting tragedy capitalize
    on me.

George Michael told me not to take things too seriously.
So, I lowered my shoulders and stretched my smile with a sewing
    kit.

I remember when I broke into hysteria,
Like all the times I came in second to first.
I watched the oil slither, particle by particle.

Topaz.

Vitamins and Threads

i.

Looked in the mirror.
I saw somebody else.
I saw something else.

What have I done to myself?
How did I get here?
I don't like it anymore.

I need to go somewhere else.
I need to go someplace else.
I need to go away entirely.

"But I'm not ready, It's not my time." I say this every night.

I'm unrecognizable now.
Images of childhood seem unreal, intangible.
I can't associate myself with past imagery anymore,
I wasn't there before.

ii.

I'm a different person now.
I'm a different hurting now.
I'm a different yearning now.

I've been crying for years; I built a lake of tears.

I wish someone could rescue me instead, but I fear I've been left
for dead inside my bed, with my vitamins and threads beside my
coffins head, one big bright bow and my mother, she said I'd do

something great, and to her disappointment, here I lay rest at nine in the morning, lowered beneath the soil at twenty, in red clothes and my hands on my chest, wishing from these depths I could reverse time and be a better person.

I'm not ready yet.
I'm not ready yet.

My Magnum Opus

I like writing because it's the vitamins I miss, the kisses I wish,
And the leftover dish I can appreciate with my wrists.

God, it's a tightsrope; unforgiving, patient and singular.
God, it's a kite's hope; survival in the sky and perpendicular.

Dance beside me, even the four walls are giggling at four.
Take it seriously, paint the next revolution and more.
I'm happy having fun in the shades of greatness at shore.

This is my magnum opus.
This is my mother's confidence.
This is my brother hopeless,
This is my sisters focus.

Oh Mr. Harris, what a teacher.
Your cursive writing inspired me,
Believe it or not.
You wrote a goodbye note— framed it in my palms since I was 12.

All of these livelihoods we share.
All of their magnum opus's is
All of my madness under the Canopus.

Author's Note

I've been searching for solace. I've been seeking creative elevation through my life as an artist; a full-time poet. *My Magnum Opus* echoes my message through the beauty in appreciating everything. I take all of it, absorbing every emotion the human experience tests me with, as it is mine. Each moment is my pinnacle in life. Every time I am disappointed, betrayed, inspired or motivated, it is all of the same value to my existence. Everything I am given the opportunity to experience is more reason to create; more reason to reinvent. I am here until I die. I am here until my mother is no longer here, and my sisters, and my brother, and me. I am here to relish in all of it. I am here for my magnum opus.